Praying
With
Tongues of Fire

Written by Belinda K Owens

D1501693

Praying
With
Tongues of Fire

"I dedicate this book to the memory of my dad, C .W. Wood Jr
he was a man of God and blazed the trail before me"

³ And there appeared unto them cloven tongues like as of fire, and it sat upon each of them.
Acts 2:3 (KJV)

Warning!

This book can be hazardous to depression,

oppression & possession

Speaking in Tongues?

So what is speaking in tongues? Why would anyone want to? What happens when we do?

First off let me say unlike some who were raised where speaking in tongues was "taboo" I was raised where speaking in tongues was the norm. I was filled with the Holy Ghost when I was around 7 years old and have been speaking in tongues ever since. It is a special gift from God that, just like He promised, it brings great comfort.

[26] But the Comforter, which is the Holy Ghost, whom the Father will send in my name, he shall teach you all things, and bring all things to your remembrance, whatsoever I have said unto you. John 14:26

"The Gift"

This wonderful gift from God has been refused, misunderstood, and yes miss used. Jesus said that the Father God would send this comforter for us, to help us. The Holy Ghost cannot help us if we refuse to have anything to do with Him.

I have laid hands on people that were asking for the infilling of the Holy Spirit with the evidence of speaking in tongues and watched as their tongues would come forth bring great joy and yes, peace to them.

I know at Azusa Street there were reports of the building being on fire. So much so that the firemen quit going to check it out because they knew it wasn't on fire, it was God in cloven tongues just like in Acts. Acts 2:3 And there appeared unto them cloven tongues like as of fire, and it sat upon each of them.

God is so majestic, and so much greater than we can fathom! I don't know about you but I am ready for a habitation of the Father that passes anything we have experienced up to date. Some are critical of all that God is and they want to restrain you from reaching out for more. All I can say is "I have tasted and I have seen that my Lord is good! I want all of Him I can contain!"

A friend sent me a picture several years ago which was taken as he was ministering. There were tongues as of fire all above the heads of the people in the photo. God is God and not everything about Him fits into our tiny minds.

As I have said before, if we can understand everything about God than He ceases to be God.

I was in a church service in Mississippi one night and as I stood there during worship I began to see in the spirit realm. I saw angels about 30' feet tall one on each side of the platform. As the worship was going up I watched as the angels opened their mouths and blew fire out over the crowd. As this happened I saw the physical reaction that the crowd experienced because of this fire being released over us. People began weeping; worshipping, shouting and some went to their knees. I felt as though I would fall on my face in worship but I did my best to stand because I wanted to see what was happening! God was in the house!

I believe God has been rolling up His sleeves and there will be a mighty pouring out of His glory upon His children. Let's buckle in and get ready, it's about to get wild!

"A Language Spoken in the Spirit Realm"

I have been in situations where during a time of danger as I prayed concerning and addressing the danger that tongues would start rolling out of my mouth. It is a language that is spoken in the spirit realm. It crosses our earthly languages and is universal, understood by those functioning in that realm.

When I was about 13 years old my mother & dad and two of my sisters were traveling across old Mexico. We were headed down to Oaxaca at the bottom end of Mexico to hold some meetings.

As we were traveling one night just outside of Mexico City I remember that the van we were in started to spit and sputter along about the time we were passing a group of threatening looking men. As the van sputtered my dad told us "y'all better start praying because this doesn't look good." All of a sudden tongues started coming out of my mouth. As the tongues came out of me the van began to catch and run.

I continued to pray with the unction of the Holy Spirit and the van stopped its sputtering and took off down the road keeping us from harm's way.

Me, our translator Lazarus, my little sister Deanna
and the van we traveled in across Mexico

"No Language Barriers"

I have been confronted by a demon possessed person that came into our meeting and for who knows why, the person came up into the prayer line. I think demons like to try and function as close to the presence of God as they can. They like to pretend that they are a part of the presence of God but this is majorly hypocritical. We know what they are. They are sent to kill, steal, and destroy.

Let me explain here to those who may not know what a "prayer line" is. A prayer line is where people asking for those who are ministering to lay hands on them to receive from the Lord. They come up front and the ministers lay hands on them as they pray.

As I lay hands on this person they began to manifest demonically. I won't go into a full description of demon possession here, but as this person manifested I began to speak in tongues over them. As I would speak a few sentences in tongues the demon would shake the person's head saying "no". Again tongues would roll out of me commanding the demon to come out of the person by the name of Jesus and the demon would shake the person's head saying "no". So I know at that point the demonic spirit I was dealing with did understand the tongue language I was speaking. I have had this happen several times over the years while casting out demons. There is authority in speaking in tongues!

"Power has been received!"

⁸ But ye shall receive power, after that the Holy Ghost is come upon you: and ye shall be witnesses unto me both in Jerusalem, and in all Judaea, and in Samaria, and unto the uttermost part of the earth. Acts 1:8 (KJV)

There is a tongue that is understood by God. We can use it to speak with Him one on one. 1 Corinthians 14:2 (KJV) ² For he that speaketh in an unknown tongue speaketh not unto men, but unto God: for no man understandeth him; howbeit in the spirit he speaketh mysteries.

After all He has created everything why would we think it was impossible for Him to have a language designated just for Himself where He can communicate with His children one on one.

He is God and He does as He desires. Psalm 115:3 (KJV) [3] But our God is in the heavens: he hath done whatsoever he hath pleased.

"Don't Know How to Pray? Pray in Tongues"

In working with people who speak a different language than we do I find it very useful to pray over them in tongues because the Spirit of the Lord knows what the issue is where we may not. So when you engage the heavens and begin to function in a Kingdom manner, even if you can't speak the language of the people, you can still get results by letting the Holy Spirit inside of you move.

Mark 16:17 (KJV) [17] And these signs shall follow them that believe; In my name shall they cast out devils; they shall speak with new tongues;

"Let the Spirit of God fill you up so much that you over flow!"

"Holy Spirit Our Teacher"

Now let's dig a little deeper. There is no end to what we don't know about heaven, God, Kingdom, tongues, & everything else supernatural. I honestly believe that we will know so much more than we do now when we cross over, but I believe we will also realize how little we know.

^{26} But the Comforter, which is the Holy Ghost, whom the Father will send in my name, he shall teach you all things, and bring all things to your remembrance, whatsoever I have said unto you. John 14:26 (KJV)

I can only imagine what it would be like to follow Jesus around as He was demonstrating who He was.

According to this scripture it appears that we are capable of loosing things we have learned or the scripture would not have included "he will teach you everything and remind you of everything I have told you." The Holy Spirit is a wonderful teacher. He can help with your job, your school work if you are a student, your children if you are a parent, and so much more if we let Him. You might say "how is that?" Well let me challenge you. If you are facing something and you do not know what to do about it or how to handle it just ask the Father to release the Holy Spirit to help. Then listen to what the Spirit may tell you. Sometimes He speaks in a still small voice and sometimes He speaks loud like thunder.

I remember the testimony of someone who had a situation at their job. A machine was malfunctioning and nothing seemed to fix it. This person prayed and asked God to show them how to fix it. They went to sleep and had a dream. In the dream he went to work, walked in. He walked thru the plant and to where the machine was. In the dream he turned a certain direction walked a few feet and then reached over and opened a panel. Inside the panel was a switch and in the dream they flipped it.

When this person woke up the next morning and went to work, He was obedient and walked and did exactly what he had done in the dream the night before. He walked to the panel opened it up, flipped the switch and guess what? It worked! The machine was fixed! All because someone asked for help and they were obedient.

When I was 9 years old I was learning to play the drums. I would try to do runs and things on the drums but it was difficult. I found that in a church service where the Spirit of God was moving I would do runs and things on the drums I had no clue how to do. When the Spirit of the Lord was in the house I would learn new runs and hits that on my own wasn't possible. The Holy Ghost was my teacher!

"Necessity can push us into Faith"

We have witnessed miracles because someone had enough guts to ask our Father for help! Usually you see more miracles on the mission field because more help is needed there. They can't just go "buy" or "pickup" the solution to the problem. You must walk on faith when there are no other options.

The Holy Spirit is ours to use. There has been scientific evidence showing how the human brain reacts when we speak in tongues.

Research on the relationship between the brain and praying or speaking in tongues found that as we pray in the Spirit or worship in the Spirit (our heavenly language), the brain releases 2 chemical secretions that are directed into our immune systems giving a 35 to 40 percent boost to the immune system. This promotes healing within our bodies. This secretion comes from a part of the brain that has no other apparent activity in humans and is only activated by our Spirit-led prayer and worship.

So it is healthy to speak in tongues! Speaking in tongues is also associated with a reduction in stress and is associated with positive mood and calmness. I believe we should speak in tongues daily. Whether you are asking for something or you are just spending some time before the Father just let it roll out of your mouth.

Blind Eyes Can See!

This handkerchief is one my dad used to lay on two different blind eyes and saw both of them completely healed! God still wants to heal if we just release Him and act in faith!

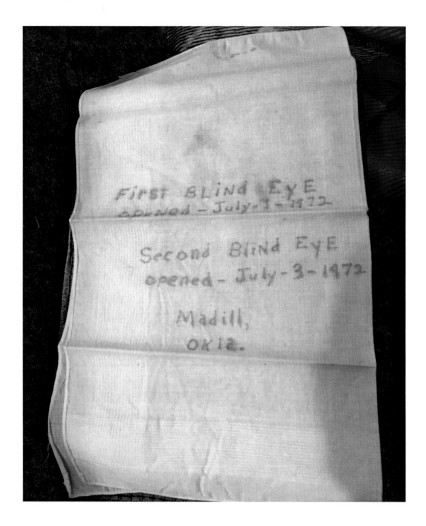

"Receiving the Holy Spirit with evidence of speaking in tongues"

2 And when the day of Pentecost was fully come, they were all with one accord in one place.

² And suddenly there came a sound from heaven as of a rushing mighty wind, and it filled all the house where they were sitting.

³ And there appeared unto them cloven tongues like as of fire, and it sat upon each of them.

⁴ And they were all filled with the Holy Ghost, and began to speak with other tongues, as the Spirit gave them utterance. Acts 2:1-4 (KJV)

They began to speak in languages they had not known before. The Spirit gave them the ability to do this.

I personally believe you have the right to heaven whether or not you speak in an unknown language. Now let me say this "why would you want to come so far and then decide you do not want the rest of what God has for you?" Receiving the Holy Spirit will give you a deeper understanding of all things God. The Holy Spirit will open up the word of God in ways you never knew before. If you have a desire as a citizen of heaven to bring heaven to earth and effect your world then you need to have this essential gifting.

After 51 years of walking with the Father and speaking in tongues I will say I would never want to be without it. Yes tongues have been misused. But so has every other aspect of Christian life. From Judas to Peter we see short comings and misconduct and we don't throw Christianity out the door. We hopefully learn from these and go on walking better than before because we now see what not to do.

I want to encourage you to ask the Lord to fill you with the Holy Spirit!

I have prayed for people to receive the infilling of the Holy Spirit and have watched the mouth and tongue quiver as their brand new heavenly language flowed out of them! That is an exciting experience! I want to admonish you that when you ask to be filled if you only hear two small words to step out on them and more will come.

I have also had people tell me that when they only spoke a few words in tongues that the next day Satan would start in telling them "Oh you didn't receive anything! You just got one or two words." When that happens tell Satan to get behind you! And then you stand on faith and continue to speak out those few words and they will grow!

I have experienced different languages over the years. My tongue has change just like my walk with the Lord has changed and grown. It is ok if your language changes.

I have a friend in Nicaragua who would speak in tongues and one day she went back to her childhood village up in the mountains and she found out that her prayer language was the language her people used to speak up in the mountains! She had no idea and did not know that language but God did!

Another experience I had in the mountains of Nicaragua was I had a pastor tell me that he had a word from the Lord for me. I said ok and we gathered around to hear the word. He spoke in tongues, then his wife interpreted it from tongues to Spanish, then our translator interpreted the Spanish to me in English! That was one of the neatest experiences. Tongues to Spanish, Spanish to English! YAY God!

"Waking with God is a wild ride"

He will not be boring. The minute you think you have Him figured out He will stand up and show you that He is so much more! I have a family member who wasn't raised in a church where speaking in tongues is accepted. They decided one night to take their friend along to a full gospel meeting where tongues were spoken just to see their reaction. Well they went to the service and a young person got up and spoke a bit in tongues. Then the young person set down. After service this family member asked their friend what they thought of the tongues that young person spoke in. The friend replied "what message in tongues?"

They said "I did not hear any tongues. That person got up and spoke to me in English about some things I was going to go thru." The friend heard English while the rest heard tongues. We forget sometimes how big our God really is! We must get out of our sandbox and see the rest of the Kingdom!

[27] But the anointing which ye have received of him abideth in you, and ye need not that any man teach you: but as the same anointing teacheth you of all things, and is truth, and is no lie, and even as it hath taught you, ye shall abide in him. 1 John 2:27(KJV)

I pray that you speak in tongues and you do so often bringing the Kingdom here. Let it flow!

"My dad holding our son Cameron"

C.W.Wood Jr.

Nov. 9, 1936 – April 26, 1995

Cameron Philip Owens

April 26, 1982 – March 3,2005

Made in United States
North Haven, CT
01 May 2022

18770720R00018

Belinda Owens has served as Sr. Pastor Lighthouse Church and multiple years in mission ministries to Latin America. She is co-founder and director of Eagle Nest Ministries based in southwest Missouri. She is the mother of two sons and the grandmother of four. She currently serves on the pastoral staff at the Glory Barn Branson, Mo. She is the author of several books from children to adults that teach Kingdom living. You can find her books at: amazon.com/author/belindaowens

ISBN 9781704381442

9 781704 381442